Under Wraps
The Gift We Never Expected

Under Wraps
The Gift We Never Expected

Book
978-1-4267-9373-8
978-1-6308-8296-9 (Large Print)
Also available as an eBook

Leader Guide
978-1-4267-9375-2
Also available as an eBook

DVD
978-1-4267-9378-3

Devotional
978-1-4267-9376-9
Also available as an eBook

Children's Leader Guide
978-1-4267-9381-3

Youth Study Book
978-1-4267-9379-0
Also available as an eBook

Worship Planning
978-1-4267-9382-0 (Flash Drive)
978-1-6308-8069-9 (Download)

Under Wraps

The Gift We Never Expected

Jessica LaGrone

Andy Nixon

Rob Renfroe

Ed Robb

Nashville
Abingdon Press

UNDER WRAPS: THE GIFT WE NEVER EXPECTED

Copyright © 2014 Abingdon Press

All rights reserved.

This book is printed on elemental chlorine-free paper.

ISBN 978-1-4267-9373-8

14 15 16 17 18 19 20 21 22 23—10 9 8 7 6 5 4 3 2 1
MANUFACTURED IN THE UNITED STATES OF AMERICA

Contents

Introduction

Introduction

"The Word became flesh and blood,
and moved into the neighborhood."
John 1:14 THE MESSAGE

The coming of Christmas is a season filled with anticipation. Often before the annual Thanksgiving meal has come and gone, we begin thinking about all that must be done in the coming weeks. We make lists and search for just the right gifts for our family, friends, and other special people we want to remember at this joyous time of year. Beautifully wrapped packages begin to appear beneath our Christmas trees adorned with twinkling lights and glimmering ornaments, seeming to cheer *It's time! It's time! Christmas is here!*

Long ago, as all of creation anticipated the first Christmas, God was getting ready to change the world through one very special gift, a gift he had planned from the very beginning:

In the beginning was the Word, and the Word was with God, and the Word was God. . . . . The Word became flesh and made his dwelling among us. We have seen his glory, the glory of the one and only Son, who came from the Father, full of grace and truth.

John 1:1,14 NIV

Just as the first wrapped gift beneath the Christmas tree heralds the arrival of a new season, so the birth of Jesus, our Savior, on Christmas Day was the first word that God's hope and salvation and redemption plan had come into the world.

The story of Christmas begins long before Jesus' birth—even before God breathed the first breath into Adam's dusty body. From the very beginning, God had a plan for redemption. The apostle Paul declared,

> *The Son is the image of the invisible God, the firstborn over all creation. . . . For God was pleased to have all his fullness dwell in him, and through him to reconcile to himself all things, whether things on earth or things in heaven, by making peace through his blood, shed on the cross.*
>
> Colossians 1:15, 19-20 NIV

From the beginning, the Bible tells of a love story between God and his people. As the story works its way through the Old Testament into the New Testament, it is a story with many ups and downs and twists and turns, but the ending is always clear—redemption is God's plan, and he will stop at nothing to fulfill that plan and rescue his people.

And so God sent Jesus. God actually gift-wrapped himself in all his fullness, in human flesh, and was born in a dusty stable so he could come and live among us and offer us life and salvation that we could never gain on our own.

Jesus is God under wraps.

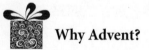 **Why Advent?**

The season of Advent—the four Sundays leading up to Christmas Day—is a special time for believers because it challenges us to pause and remember the hope we have during a stressful season that all too often emphasizes greed and money. Advent allows us the time and space to refocus our hearts and minds on Jesus—the true hope of the season.

The observation of Advent is a gift—a time to reflect, meditate, and pray, asking God to do a great work in our hearts as we remember anew the great gift that has been given to us through his Son. We observe Advent because God expects something amazing to happen in our lives at Christmas.

The theme of *Under Wraps* reflects how the character of God, communicated through the Old Testament, is revealed completely and perfectly in Jesus. Together we will see specifically how four characteristics of God—

God is expectant;
God is dangerous;
God is jealous;
God is faithful

—are described in the Old Testament and then revealed through Jesus and the time he spent here on earth.

Jesus—God under wraps—took on human flesh and came to live among us to show us who God is and what he is like. And he came on a mission—to rescue us and redeem us so that we could fully know God and be known by him.

Each week we will explore one of these four characteristics of God, shown first through the Old Testament and then revealed clearly through Jesus. Each chapter contains questions for reflection, Scriptures for meditation, and a prayer intended to assist you in reflecting on what God is doing in your heart during this season.

Whether you read these chapters on your own or as part of the *Under Wraps* group study, may this exploration of "God under wraps" enrich and prepare you spiritually as you move through the Advent season and anticipate the birth of Christ our Savior. Embrace this season of Advent expectantly, grabbing hold of the hope that is come—because God expects Christmas to change you. That is why he sent a Savior, born to change the world. That is why he gave us the gift of himself, wrapped up in Jesus Christ.

1.
God Is Expectant

1.

God Is Expectant

Jessica LaGrone

For to us a child is born,
to us a son is given,
and the government will be on his shoulders.
And he will be called
Wonderful Counselor, Mighty God,
Everlasting Father, Prince of Peace.
Of the greatness of his government and peace
there will be no end.
He will reign on David's throne
and over his kingdom,
establishing and upholding it
with justice and righteousness
from that time on and forever.
The zeal of the Lord *Almighty*
will accomplish this.

Isaiah 9:6–7 NIV

There is so much to love about the Christmas season—the colorful decorations, the festive music, the fun parties, the yummy food, and, of course, the television Christmas specials. I have loved classics like *Rudolph the Red-Nosed Reindeer, Frosty the Snowman, The Grinch Who Stole Christmas,* and *A Charlie Brown Christmas,* with that cute, sad little tree, since I was a child. This year I was excited to share these Christmas specials with my own children, so my husband and I set the DVR to record all the specials that were coming on. Imagine our surprise to find that there were two hundred eighty-five programs available!

I was relieved to find all the classics there, but there were also all kinds of other characters getting into the spirit, too—Shrek, Elmo, Mickey Mouse, Bugs Bunny, Barbie, and even Lady Gaga and The Muppets, just to name a few. It makes me laugh to think about what Charles Dickens might have to say about all the ways his story *A Christmas Carol* has been altered over the years. I'm guessing he didn't anticipate his tale would one day include mice and puppets and ogres.

Though Christmastime increasingly offers a barrage of different Christmas stories and specials, how reassuring to know that the *real, true* story of Christmas has not changed since it was written thousands of years ago. The original Christmas story is told in each of the Gospels—Matthew, Mark, Luke, and John—and though each Gospel writer's story is about a baby and a manger and shepherds and wise men, each writer tells the story a bit differently.

Surprisingly, Luke's Gospel doesn't start out with shepherds or angels or even wise men gathered around a nativity. Luke begins his Gospel with an expectant mother—but not the one we might anticipate. There's no pregnant teenager at the outset of the Gospel of Luke; instead we find a very mature woman named Elizabeth. Elizabeth has been married for decades to her husband, Zechariah, a priest. She had dreamed for many years of being a mother, but now she's no longer in the age bracket that expects little bundles of joy to arrive. And yet, here in Luke's Christmas special, Elizabeth unexpectedly finds herself expecting a baby.

Instead of hot flashes, she's getting morning sickness. It's an amazing miracle that's happening to her, and God has special plans for the baby growing inside her; he will be the prophet known as John the Baptist, and he will point the way to the coming Messiah.

Then, when Elizabeth's much younger cousin Mary comes to visit, Elizabeth takes one look at her and, without the two even exchanging a word, knows that Mary is expecting too. Immediately Elizabeth knows something very special about Mary's baby:

At that time Mary got ready and hurried to a town in the hill country of Judea, where she entered Zechariah's home and greeted Elizabeth. When Elizabeth heard Mary's greeting, the baby leaped in her womb, and Elizabeth was filled with the Holy Spirit. In a loud voice she exclaimed: "Blessed are you among women, and blessed is the child you will bear! But why am I so favored that the mother of my Lord should come to me? As soon as the sound of your greeting reached my ears, the baby in my womb leaped for joy. Blessed is she who has believed that the Lord would fulfill his promises to her."

Luke 1:39-45 NIV

That joyful greeting between these two women must have been followed by all kinds of questions. How could Elizabeth be pregnant at such an advanced age? How could Mary—a virgin—be pregnant at all? What was happening with all these angels showing up and announcing things? They must have been breathless at all the amazing things happening in their lives.

Mary and Elizabeth couldn't have been at two more different stages of life. Anti-acne cream meets anti-wrinkle serum. And yet here they are, both in the same wonderful and unexpected condition. And in all their surprise and wonder, there must also have been much rejoicing in their hearts, for the person they had been expecting for so long—God's promised Messiah—was on his way.

The Waiting Game

God's people—the people of Israel—had been waiting for the arrival of this special person for thousands of years. Now that's a long time to be expecting! God's people were waiting on one special hero—the Messiah, the Anointed One—who would show up and rescue them all. The gift of the Messiah had been forecast and broadcast and advertised for so long that people had their hopes up pretty high. The prophet Isaiah had written the prophecy,

> For to us a child is born, / to us a son is given, / and the government will be on his shoulders. / And he will be called / Wonderful Counselor, Mighty God, / Everlasting Father, Prince of Peace. / Of the greatness of his government and peace / there will be no end. / He will reign on David's throne / and over his kingdom, / establishing and upholding it / with justice and righteousness / from that time on and forever. / The zeal of the LORD Almighty / will accomplish this.
>
> Isaiah 9:6-7 NIV

The people had imagined great things about this Messiah—that he would be strong and politically powerful and exceptionally wealthy. That he would ride into Jerusalem in a chariot of fire, overthrow the oppressive Roman Empire, and place their people in power over all the other nations. Prince of Peace, Almighty God, Wonderful Counselor, great leader. No pressure, right?

In addition to their expectations, the people of God had been waiting for this Messiah for a long, long time. They had put all of their hopes and dreams into the arrival of this hero. But still no birth announcement had arrived. No Messiah had come.

Like the barren Elizabeth, they must have almost given up hope that their dreams would ever come to fruition. The years of waiting had been long, and it was getting harder and harder for the people to fight the disappointment of their unfulfilled dreams. The knowledge that the Messiah was about to be born would have been thrilling to them. But the arrival of Jesus, the Messiah, would turn out to be nothing like the people expected.

The circumstances of his humble birth were surprising, to say the least. The people of Israel were thinking palaces, not stables. They were hoping for crowns, not swaddling clothes. But Jesus' birth would only be the first of many ways that he defied everyone's expectations. Jesus was a Messiah who didn't match expectations. He was a friend to sinners. He sought out those who were the least, the lost, and the very people that everyone else had given up on. Instead of conquering those who challenged him, he died on their cross. And then he transcended all conceivable expectations by defeating death itself and rising again.

Jesus went off script, and the people of Israel didn't know what to make of him. I mean, who shows up with enough power in just his little finger to zap all the bad guys out there but then lays down his life for them instead? They expected a leader who would ride into town on a white horse and destroy their enemies, not the humble man who sauntered into town on a donkey. They wanted deliverance from their enemies—he came to deliver them from themselves.

As it always turns out, God's plans are better than anything we can ever hope for or expect. God's people expected this Messiah to be a *lot* of things, but they never expected him to be God himself. They thought God would send a messenger, a representative to save them and defeat their enemies. No one had any idea that God would show up in person. They had heard the words of the prophet Isaiah predicting that the Messiah would be miraculously born to a virgin, and that he would be known as Immanuel (Isaiah 7:14), but they were still surprised when the birth of Jesus Christ fulfilled that prophecy: "All this took place to fulfill what the Lord had said through the prophet: 'The virgin will conceive and give birth to a son, and they will call him Immanuel' (which means 'God with us')" (Matthew 1:22-23 NIV).

Immanuel. God with us. The birth of Jesus confirmed that God had not abandoned his people, that he hadn't forgotten them. In fact, he had stepped into a human body to join them in person, God in the flesh.

Jesus was the gift everyone needed but no one expected.

The Perfect Gift

Isn't it is a great feeling to find the perfect present for someone you love? You buy the gift, wrap it, and then hide it in a closet or put it under the tree, eagerly awaiting the big reveal on Christmas Day. You are expectant and eager, excited to give such a good gift to someone about whom you care deeply.

Imagine God as that expectant giver, just waiting on that first Christmas morning, holding in his hand the gift of Jesus Christ, knowing since the beginning of time that Jesus would step into history and turn it upside down (see Colossians 1:15-17; Revelation 13:8). This was it. This was the moment—God's master plan to change everything, launched on Christmas Day in the form of a tiny little baby. And even though the world was longing for him the way Elizabeth had longed for a child, like Mary, they were still surprised—completely taken off guard—when he came in the flesh.

The Gospel of John describes the arrival of Jesus: "The Word became flesh and made his dwelling among us" (John 1:14 NIV). In sending Jesus to earth, God made his Word tangible for us—something we could see and touch and hear. But he didn't stop there. In the Greek, "made his dwelling among us" is the word *skenoo*, which literally means "tabernacled"—to put up a tent, to go camping, to pitch your tent.[1] If you were Greek and you were going camping and somebody said, "Where are you going to stay?" you would say, "I'm going to *skenoo*. I'm going to pitch my tent there." And that was God's plan in Jesus. The Word became flesh—Jesus put on a tent of human flesh and moved into our camp, stepping into the terrain of human life to show us the way.

Several years ago I experienced what it means for others to step into our own journeys when I had the very distinct privilege of being the first pregnant pastor my church had ever known. It seemed that everyone in the church was really excited about this pregnancy. It was a community event; we were all expecting together. There was a lot of "we" language happening. Members would say things like, "Do we know if it's a boy or a girl?" "Do we have a name for the baby yet?" If you're close to someone who's about to deliver a baby, it's natural for you get excited about it. You're on pins and needles. You have your cell phone on, ready to answer that call, respond to that text, rush to the hospital. You're checking social media to see if there's any update. And if there's not, you text: "How's it going?" "What's happening?" "When is our baby gonna get here?"

It was Christmastime toward the end of my pregnancy, and I was certainly "great with child," which I discovered makes a lot of people very nervous. I worked up until the day my son was born, and so there I was in the office every day, people watching me like a hawk. It was a very strange feeling. One day I stepped out of my office for a moment, and one of our pastors walked by my office and stopped.

"Jessica's not in her office!" he said to whomever was nearby. "Is she okay? Do you think she's in labor?"

When a baby is on the way, the sense of expectancy is catching, and that is exactly what the Advent season should be like for believers. In these weeks leading up to Christmas, our sense of expectancy should spread like wildfire. We should be excited to embrace that beautiful "we" language. *We* can't wait for Christmas to get here. *We* can't wait to celebrate this baby's birth. *We* can't wait to share him with the world because we know the promise that the birth of Jesus brings. This is *our* baby, *our* season. And we share our expectancy with a world who desperately hope for something they can't quite understand. Even among unbelievers the Christmas season brings a sense of hope that the unchangeable can change, that good can prevail over evil. Though some might not understand the *true* reason for the season, they express these God-given feelings in other ways—like creating a family Christmas special where twelve puppies save Christmas from disaster or Mickey finds the perfect, selfless gift for Minnie.

We expectantly hope for redemption, and we do not hope in vain, for God's plan was for Christmas to change the world. And when it comes around this time of year, every year, we can again celebrate the hope that the arrival of this baby means something, that Christmas does change the world. Because the birth of Christ is the hinge of history, the moment when the world experienced the hope that would forever change everything; and our yearly observance of Advent is a reminder of the hope that Jesus brought with him into this world.

The Gift that Changes Everything

What are you expecting for Christmas this year? What are your hopes for the season? Do you expect Christmas to change anything, really?

Most of us will likely observe the same family traditions and pull out the same decorations. We'll eat meals with the same family members. We'll get what seems like the same gifts over and over again from the same people. The same family members will likely be fighting about the same things as last year. The old, familiar phrases will come out. For example, I can predict in the next week and a half that my grandmother, who is ninety-three years old, will come to each of us in the family, privately and secretly, and say something like, "Now, honey, it's gonna be a lean Christmas this year. Don't expect much." She has said that to me every Christmas of my entire life, and she always gives lavishly and generously. It never fails.

Do you expect anything to change for you this Christmas? Maybe not, but God does. Because that is what the season is about. Because even when the Christmas season seems predictable and stale, the full realization of the birth of Christ can breathe life into even the hardest of hearts.

There is one Christmas story that radio broadcaster Paul Harvey used to tell every Christmas season about a man who just didn't believe in Christmas.[2] His wife got the kids ready to go to church for Christmas Eve services and asked him to come along, but the man—a farmer—refused to go with them.

"Well, why would I want to get all dressed up in a scratchy suit and go sit in that to church with people I don't even like and sing about a God I don't even believe exists?" he grumbled.

After the wife and kids left for church, the farmer heard a noise in the dining room. He ran in and saw that a little bird had flown into the dining room window. It had hit the window and bounced off and was lying there, stunned, in the flowerbed. Then the man noticed that a whole flock of small birds was in his yard, unusual for that time of year. Apparently they had been caught in an early snowfall and had to land right there in his pasture. They weren't meant to be out there in the cold; and the farmer knew if they stayed out there, they might freeze to death.

Concerned, the farmer tried to lure the birds into his warm barn for shelter. He went out and opened the doors of the barn, but the birds didn't pay any attention. He turned on the light and tried to make it warm and inviting, but the birds didn't even notice. He tried making a trail of feed from the inside of the barn all the way out to where most of the birds were. But they simply pecked at the seed and wouldn't get anywhere close to him. He tried to chase them into the barn. But nothing worked; they didn't understand they needed to go into the barn for safety and shelter.

Discouraged, the farmer dropped to his knees in the snow. And then it hit him. *The only way I can get through to them is to be a bird,* he thought. *To become like them, to put on a cloak of feathers, become one of them, and tell them about the hope, the life, the salvation that rests just on the other side of the barn doors. If only.*

Suddenly he remembered where his wife and children were—down at the little church, celebrating a little baby who came into the world to offer the hope the whole world needed. Who came to offer *him* life and hope.

The story's been told many times and in many different ways, but I love the ending where that farmer puts on a scratchy suit, drives down the road, slides into the pew next to his very surprised wife, and begins to sing more loudly than anyone in the church: *"Praise be to the newborn king, Christ our Lord"; "Silent night, holy night. Son of God, love's pure light."* The farmer began to believe that something could change because of Christmas.

Once when I told this story to a group of teenagers who had just heard it for the first time, they were quiet. As I closed, I said that we should pray together for those people in our lives who don't know Jesus.

"Who is the farmer for you, that one who doesn't know the gift of Jesus Christ?" I asked them. "Who is your heart breaking for—someone you want to know the gift of Jesus this Christmas, who hasn't recognized that God came in person for them. Who do you want God to get through to this Christmas?"

And they began to pray. One said the name of a teacher, another the name of her friend. And that's when it started. The next one said, "My dad."

And the one after her said, "My dad." And then it just kept going. *My dad, my dad, my dad.* I thought I knew these kids really well, but I didn't know that their hearts were breaking for the men they looked up to more than anyone in the world to look up to the God that they loved. And what broke me is that when I was their age, I had prayed that same prayer. *My dad.*

Many of us have prayed with full hearts for those we love to find the strength and comfort that comes from knowing Jesus Christ. Are you praying for God to reach in and change the life of someone you love this Christmas? It's a risky prayer. To have enough hope that Christmas will reach a reluctant heart is a prayer that is pregnant, expectant with hope.

Christmas happened because God expected to change the world, to give hope where there was none. God the Father, wrapped in mystery throughout the Old Testament, revealed himself to us in a whole new way through the birth of Jesus Christ, stepping into our midst and forever changing our understanding of his love and grace.

What are you expecting this Christmas? Do you have a longing that God will change something in our world? That God will change someone you love? That God will change *you*? God loves an expectant heart, and he is eager to surprise us with the gifts of his goodness and love. May we wait for him with eager hearts.

Reflect

As we enter into the Advent season, where is your heart? Like Elizabeth, are you filled with longing? Like Mary, are you reeling with uncertainty? How might refocusing your heart to expectantly await Jesus' coming—the moment everything changed and God came for us—affect the way you enter into this season?

_____

_____

_____

_____

_____

Christmas was God's master plan to change the world in a way that no one expected. How has Jesus defied your expectations? Where might hope be leading you?

_____

_____

_____

_____

_____

Meditate

And Mary said:

"My soul glorifies the Lord
    and my spirit rejoices in God my Savior,
for he has been mindful
    of the humble state of his servant.
From now on all generations will call me blessed,
    for the Mighty One has done great things for me—
    holy is his name.
His mercy extends to those who fear him,
    from generation to generation.
He has performed mighty deeds with his arm;
    he has scattered those who are proud in their inmost thoughts.
He has brought down rulers from their thrones
    but has lifted up the humble.
He has filled the hungry with good things
    but has sent the rich away empty.
He has helped his servant Israel,
    remembering to be merciful
to Abraham and his descendants forever,
    just as he promised our ancestors."

Luke 1:46-55 NIV

On this mountain the LORD of hosts will make for all peoples
    a feast of rich food, a feast of well-aged wines,
    of rich food filled with marrow, of well-aged wines strained clear. . . .

*Then the Lord G*OD *will wipe away the tears from all faces,*
 and the disgrace of his people he will take away from all the earth,
 *for the L*ORD *has spoken.*
It will be said on that day,
 Lo, this is our God; we have waited for him, so that he might save us.
 *This is the L*ORD *for whom we have waited;*
 let us be glad and rejoice in his salvation.

Isaiah 25:6, 8-9 NRSV

The Lord is near. Do not worry about anything, but in everything by prayer and supplication with thanksgiving let your requests be made known to God. And the peace of God, which surpasses all understanding, will guard your hearts and your minds in Christ Jesus.

Philippians 4:5b-7 NRSV

Pray

God, I'm grateful that you loved us enough to put on flesh, to come and pitch your tent beside us, to become a vulnerable baby. And Lord, I love that you want Christmas to change the world. So change the world, God. Start with me. I pray for those people who are on my heart who might not even know why you came, God. I pray for those closest to me, for those I have hoped against all hope will change. And I pray, God, that you will change those things in my heart that have seemed unchangeable. I love you, Jesus. I am expectant for you. Amen.

2.
God Is Dangerous

2.
Qod Is Dangerous

Ed Robb

For God so loved the world that he gave his one and only Son, that whoever believes in him shall not perish but have eternal life. For God did not send his Son into the world to condemn the world, but to save the world through him. Whoever believes in him is not condemned, but whoever does not believe stands condemned already because they have not believed in the name of God's one and only Son. This is the verdict: Light has come into the world, but people loved darkness instead of light because their deeds were evil. . . . Whoever believes in the Son has eternal life, but whoever rejects the Son will not see life, for God's wrath remains on them.

John 3:16–19, 36 NIV

When was the last time you held a newborn baby in your arms? It's an amazing experience, isn't it? What words came to mind when you held that tiny baby?

One word that always comes to my mind when I hold a baby is *precious*, because the birth of a baby is such an amazing gift. We know the science of conception and pregnancy and birth, but all that can't fully explain the miracle of new life. *Tiny* and *cute* are other words that often come to mind. Such little fingers and nose and ears. Sometimes upon hearing the news of a new baby, the word that immediately comes to mind is *surprise*. Maybe this wasn't the plan, but *voilà*! A baby is born, and mom and dad just can't imagine life without the new addition to the family.

The news of Jesus' birth was certainly a surprise—maybe more like a shock—for Mary and Joseph. They were just good Jewish kids, minding their p's and q's, when the news of a baby came like a bombshell into their lives. *Surprise!* They weren't prepared. They hadn't planned on something like this happening to them, but God was certainly not surprised. Christ's birth had been planned since the time of Adam and Eve—since our first human parents turned away from God and away from God's perfect plan, since they rebelled against the Creator and fell under the curse of sin.

Precious. Tiny. Cute. All perfect descriptions of a newborn. But how about *dangerous*? Has that ever come to your mind as you've held a brand-new baby? Though Jesus surely must not have seemed dangerous to his mother and father and the shepherds who came to see him—a tiny thing wrapped and swaddled and lying in a manger—this baby was different. This baby was God in the flesh—the King of kings, Lord of lords, Ruler of all; the all-powerful, eternal Creator himself, sent to walk the earth among human beings, with a dangerous mission in mind.

The Dangerous Nature of God

The Bible tells us that God is dangerous—dangerous because he's a mighty God with powerful plans and expectations for his children. Not that God is manipulative, with ill will toward his wayward creation, or that his plans are to harm us; quite the contrary. God is the King of kings who wants to see the best for his people, the Lord of lords who wants to protect his children, and the Ruler of all who wants to bring all people into his kingdom. God so loved the world that he calls us to live our lives to the fullest, which sometimes means we are called to tasks we never imagined ourselves undertaking, to challenges we feel ill equipped to handle, and to unknown territory where we may not want to go. Time and time again we find God calling his people into roles they had not imagined, challenges they resisted, and dangerous territories they had not anticipated.

In Genesis 12, God called Abraham to leave "your country, your people, and your father's household" (v. 1 NIV). At the time Abraham did not see the master plan that God had for his life, nor could he imagine the blessings that lay ahead. He had to rely on faith and the promises of God and travel into unknown territory. Surely God's call on his life must have seemed dangerous.

I am certain Moses considered God dangerous as well. He was minding his own business, tending his father-in-law's sheep, when God commissioned him into service through a burning bush: " 'I am sending you to Pharaoh to bring my people the Israelites out of Egypt.' But Moses said to God, 'Who am I that I should go to Pharaoh and bring the Israelites out of Egypt?' " (Exodus 3:10-11 NIV). Remember that Moses was wanted for murder back in Egypt. Returning would be a dangerous assignment. He felt ill equipped to lead a nation or to speak for God, and yet he was called to follow the path the Lord set out in front of him; and he did, choosing to put his life in God's hands.

Jonah knew something about the dangerous nature of God. God called Jonah to "Go to the great city of Nineveh and preach against it, because its wickedness has come up before me" (Jonah 1:2 NIV), but Jonah feared his calling and ran away from the Lord. He didn't want the people of Nineveh to experience God's forgiveness, love, and mercy because they were his enemies. But God had a fishy way of getting Jonah's attention and then redirecting him back to the purpose for which he was called, and Jonah finally obeyed.

In Scripture God continually pushed those he called into dangerous situations, but he always equipped them with his power and protection to carry out the difficult tasks they were called to do. While they probably would not have volunteered for these God-sized tasks, in the end they accomplished them with God's help.

The dangerous God we follow calls us out of our prejudices and our fears. Once we have decided to follow him, he calls us to fully trust in him. While we may have wandered our own paths before meeting God, he leads us in paths of righteousness for his name's sake (see Psalm 23:3). Abraham was surrounded by non-believers in the midst of a culture that grasped at every false god available, but the one true God changed his name and used him to make a nation of believers. Moses was afraid of his own shortcomings, but God blessed him and used him to free his chosen people. Jonah wasn't willing to go where he was called, but God pursued him and used him to take the Word of God to a disobedient people.

From the beginning of time, God has been a mighty God, calling his children to stretch beyond what they are capable of on their own in order to restore his relationship with them. We need to realize that putting ourselves at the mercy of God's dangerous call is actually the safest place of all, since it puts us in the middle of his perfect will.

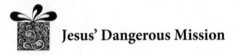 **Jesus' Dangerous Mission**

Even Jesus found himself in the midst of God's perfect will with a dangerous mission to accomplish.

It's no overstatement to say that the birth of Jesus shook up the world. That night, while the heavenly choirs sang, "Glory to God in the highest heaven, / and on earth peace to those on whom his favor rests!" (Luke 2:14 NIV), there was a shudder in hell. While the shepherds worshiped at the manger and Mary's heart leapt with joy, there was fear in the dark regions below. Yes, Satan's followers quaked with terror when Christ was born in Bethlehem. His coming was dangerous for them, because he came with a sword of truth and righteousness aimed directly at them; and he came to end their dark rule. Jesus said, "Do not suppose that I have come to bring peace to the earth. I did not come to bring peace, but a sword" (Matthew 10:34 NIV).

With our scientific, practical minds, it is often hard for us to acknowledge or give weight to the spiritual battle that is ever going on around us.

It's easy for us to presume that all that exists is the physical world we can see and touch and feel—those things we can measure and explain and test in some laboratory. But the Bible tells us that there is another realm beyond this physical world, beyond our five senses; and just because we cannot touch it or see it or measure it does not make it any less real. The Bible says that in this spiritual realm there is a cosmic battle raging—a colossal struggle between the forces of light and darkness, truth and deception, good and evil—and that we are swept into the fight. The apostle Paul wrote, "For our struggle is not against flesh and blood, but against the rulers, against the authorities, against the powers of this dark world and against the spiritual forces of evil in the heavenly realms" (Ephesians 6:12 NIV).

There are powers beyond what we can see or feel or touch or measure that threaten our well-being—powers that propagate injustice and spread destruction and lies across this world. It all began in Genesis. Adam and Eve walked together in the garden, living in perfect communion with God. Creation was in balance, in perfect harmony. There was a oneness between humanity and nature, a closeness with humanity and God. And then Satan, the one the Bible calls the "father of lies" (John 8:44 NRSV) and a deceiver (Revelation 12:9 NRSV), appeared as a serpent, whispering lies to them, casting a shadow over all of God's goodness. "Did God really tell you that you could not eat the fruit of the tree? Are you being denied? Why would God tell you this? Don't you want to be like God?" he whispered (see Genesis 3).

This voice of lies still pursues us today. The Bible warns that he "prowls around like a roaring lion looking for someone to devour" (1 Peter 5:8 NIV). This evil one, this fallen angel, has been in conflict with God eons before time began, pushing against the Creator. And his followers are still working to bring chaos and upheaval and turmoil in this world—still trying to destroy our relationship with our Creator. From the beginning, Satan has whispered in our ears, causing discontent and casting doubt in our hearts. Those lies have captured our minds and caused devastation in our lives, and the result of believing those lies is always deep separation from the one who made us. That is why Jesus came. That is why God humbled himself and entered our time and space. The Bible says Jesus came "to destroy the works of the devil" (1 John 3:8 NRSV).

Jesus is dangerous, all right. He is dangerous to the forces of darkness because he came to usher in a new era when sin would lose its grip on humanity and death would no longer have the last word. Jesus was born into this world to bring light to the darkness. In John's Gospel we see that God sent his only Son, and "In him was life, and that life was the light of all mankind. The light shines in the darkness" (John 1:4-5 NIV). Jesus also came to fight against injustice and to destroy the works of the devil, not only in the spiritual realm but here on earth as well. The prophet Isaiah proclaimed the good work that would come from Christ, that through his faithfulness and power he would establish justice on earth (see Isaiah 42).

On a cosmic level, Jesus came not only to thwart the spiritual battles that we fight daily, but also to turn the battle on its head. Jesus won the battle at Calvary, the decisive battle for all of history. We live in the period between Christ's victory on the cross and the final consummation of the war, and so the last gasp of evil has not yet been heard; but Christ continues to make advances for the kingdom and to call us into battle with him. As we fight for the purposes of God, we need to remember that good is never a lost cause since the battle has already been won on the cross.

The demons weren't the only ones shaking on the day that Christ was born. The notion of the birth of a powerful ruler did not sit well with a wicked king. The book of Matthew tells us,

> *Now after Jesus was born in Bethlehem of Judea in the days of Herod the king, behold, wise men from the East came to Jerusalem, saying, "Where is He who has been born King of the Jews? For we have seen His star in the East and have come to worship Him." When Herod the king heard* this, *he was troubled.*
>
> Matthew 2:1-3 NKJV

Troubled. It's a little preposterous to think that a powerful king like Herod—often known in history as Herod the Great—would be afraid of an infant. Herod was a king of great influence and accomplishment. In fact, many of the amazing structures that he commissioned and built—aqueducts, theaters, fortresses such as Masada—still stand in Israel, evoking style and grandeur.[1] Herod was one of the great builders of all the ancient world. He was all-powerful, rich, dominant, feared, ruthless. He tolerated no one who would challenge him, even murdering his own wife and two of his sons. Behind this powerful man was a frightened man. And so when rumors came of the birth of a new king, a king who had been prophesied and foretold from old, Herod was troubled, all right—so much so that he ordered all the infant boys in Bethlehem murdered.

Even as a babe, Jesus was dangerous to Herod, because Jesus' coming was a trumpet blast from heaven announcing that injustice would not go unchallenged; that the tyrants who built their empires by tramping on the rights of ordinary men and women would finally face a day of reckoning; that the privileged few at the top who ignored the cries of the needy would face divine judgment. Scripture says, "The LORD is slow to anger but great in power; / the LORD will not leave the guilty unpunished. . . . The earth trembles at his presence, / the world and all who live in it" (Nahum 1:3, 5 NIV).

Most of us prefer to think of Jesus in light of his compassion. We remember that he did not turn away the children who followed him: "Do not hinder them," he said, "for the kingdom of God belongs to such as these" (Mark 10:14 NIV). We recall that he healed the man who was blind (see John 9) and the woman who was sick (see Matthew 9). We like to remember all the times Jesus showed compassion and love to those around him. All of this is true of his character.

There's also another side of Jesus: he had the capacity for righteous anger. When he found that the Pharisees were more concerned with the letter of the law than a man who needed healing, Jesus became angry (see Mark 3:1-6). When he saw religious leaders abuse God's law for their own purposes, he became angry (see Matthew 15:3). When he went to the Temple and saw the moneychangers taking advantage of the poor people who came to worship, he became angry and overthrew their tables, saying: "It is written, 'My house will be called a house of prayer,' but you are making it 'a den of robbers' " (Matthew 21:13 NIV).

Jesus' birth flipped the culture's established order on its head, for he was born not in a castle but in a stable. He wore not a crown but a carpenter's belt. To most, he was an unlikely teacher, an unlikely king. He was a threat to all the unjust power systems that existed, and he challenged their reign of corruption with his perfect justice and divine grace. He still does today.

Expect the Unexpected

An encounter with the living God is a dangerous thing—it's dangerous for those who oppose him, but it is also dangerous for those who love him and follow him. It was for Mary and Joseph, an unmarried couple with a baby on the way. Mary's pregnancy was scandalous for them and their families, but they were willing to trust God and obey his plan, and they placed their reputations on the line in order to receive the blessing God gave them. Dangerous stuff.

It was dangerous for the disciples, who dropped their nets to follow the unconventional rabbi who threatened the very nature of their culture. But the disciples gave up everything to go out with him and to heal the sick and to preach the good news.

It is dangerous for you and for me as well, because Jesus expects his followers to join with him in his work here on earth. He expects us to become agents of his truth and love and to bring light and life into the dark places of this world. When Jesus faced his disciples after the resurrection, he challenged them to take his light into the world and to continue his teaching, saying, "As the Father has sent me, I am sending you" (John 20:21 NIV). Today God continues to send his church out into unknown territory and into challenging situations, both near and far; and God equips us to take that light as he equipped the early church, offering his power through the Holy Spirit to be witnesses to the ends of the earth (see Acts 1). An encounter with Jesus is always dangerous because he has big things in mind for us, and it's probably going to be more than we ever dreamed of or expected.

Not long ago I decided that we needed to put a TV in our upstairs family room, so off I went to the store.

"Do you want LED or plasma?" the sales clerk asked me.

"Um . . . I don't know. I just want one that will fit into my cabinet," I replied.

At this point I should have realized I was in over my head in this whole endeavor, since it turns out they don't even make TVs in that size anymore. If we wanted a TV, we needed to alter our cabinet to make room for it. My wife agreed to tackle the project, so a carpenter began work on the cabinet. After the new cabinet was stained, the room needed to be repainted because, well, the existing color just didn't fit with the new stain, and then suddenly a newly reupholstered ottoman appeared in the room—to match the new drapes that were being made, of course. Decorators were consulted and workers called in. Thus set off a chain of events that eventually led to our whole house being spruced up and redecorated, all because of my desire to make one little change.

It can be dangerous to start a new project. And there is nothing more dangerous than letting God start a project in you because when you open the door of your heart to him, he will do something bigger than you ever anticipated. Too often we invite Christ into our lives wanting just a little touch-up here and there—maybe a fresh coat of paint or some new drapes. But Christ isn't into remodeling; he is in the restoration business. He won't be satisfied until he shapes you into his image. He is not willing to leave you in your marred and broken condition. As we are reassured in Scripture, "God has chosen you from the beginning for salvation through sanctification by the Spirit and faith in the truth" (2 Thessalonians 2:13 NASB). That is why he sent Jesus.

Have you ever been to the Vatican? The great works of art that are on display there are breathtaking. One of the masterpieces on display is Michelangelo's *Pietà*, a marble statue of Mary holding Jesus after he was crucified. In 1972 it was vandalized by a deranged man who attacked it with a hammer, smashing it and destroying the original beauty that Michelangelo created. Vatican artists immediately began working to repair it. Slowly, over several years, they patiently, painstakingly worked on this scarred masterpiece, recreating and restoring the statue to near-perfect condition.[2]

That's exactly what God wants to do in your life and mine—to recreate and restore our lives that have been scarred by the fallen world and the work of the devil. But being recreated and restored by Jesus is dangerous.

It doesn't mean he wants to just polish us up and tweak a few minor things here and there. When we invite Jesus into our lives, he wants to restore us to the original beauty he created; and that requires commitment and submission to the work of the Spirit of God, which pushes and pulls us as we are transformed.

In his book *Mere Christianity*, C. S. Lewis writes,

> *Imagine yourself as a living house. God comes in to rebuild that house. At first, perhaps, you can understand what He is doing. He is getting the drains right and stopping the leaks in the roof and so on: you knew that those jobs need doing and so you are not surprised. But presently he starts knocking the house about in a way that hurts abominably and does not seem to make sense. What on earth is He up to? The explanation is that He is building quite a different house from the one you thought of—throwing out a new wing here, putting on an extra floor there, running up towers, making courtyards. You thought you were going to be made into a decent little cottage: but He is building a palace. He intends to come and live in it Himself.*[3]

God's work in our lives doesn't always feel comfortable. Sometimes it doesn't make sense. Sometimes it hurts. Why put us through these renovations? Because God intends to come and reside there. That's what he's doing in our lives. The King wants to move in. And he's got work to do.

Isn't it staggering to know that our Creator loves us so much that he took on human flesh and came and lived among us? Why? To save us from our sins. To redeem our lives. To fully restore us. Jesus said, "I have come that they may have life, and have it to the full" (John 10:10 NIV). And his relentless love won't stop until we have experienced just that.

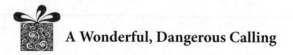 **A Wonderful, Dangerous Calling**

Christ is dangerous because he wants more for you than you've wanted for yourself, because he has higher ambitions for you than you've thought of, because he has bolder dreams than you've dared to dream. So often we want Jesus to come into our lives and work because we see him as someone who can make our lives nicer and more comfortable and pleasant. We want someone to look out for us, to make us feel better and happier. And God says, "Yes, I can do that. But I want more."

Hafiz, a Persian poet of the fourteenth century, said, "Love wants to reach out and manhandle us, break all our teacup talk of God."[4] Love sometimes gets tired of speaking sweetly and wants to rip all our erroneous notions of truth to shreds. The Beloved sometimes want to do us a great favor by holding us upside down and shaking all the nonsense out. You see, God wants to change our lives more than we sometimes are willing to accept. And for that very reason, God is dangerous. Jesus didn't come just to smooth out the wrinkles in your life but to refashion you into his image. And that will make *us* dangerous too. Jesus wants us to become dangerous tools in his hand for the good of the world.

German pastor and theologian Dietrich Bonhoeffer was, to many, a dangerous man. Considered a major threat to Adolph Hitler and the Nazi regime, he was taken as a political prisoner, carefully guarded, and tortured.[5] Why would a pastor, a theologian, be considered very dangerous to the regime? As the Nazi party gained power and legitimacy in Germany, it began to exercise power over the German church and forced many into loyalty to the Fatherland and its mission. Many came to salute the *fürher*, but not Bonhoeffer. He refused.[6] He could not look the other way. He could not remain silent in the face of such evil. Bonhoeffer led in the Resistance Movement, preaching against Nazi hatred and racism.[7] He was part of the minority in the church who bravely stood forth and said that the cross of Christ is not for sale, and the manger is not to be kidnapped and used for propaganda. And so Hitler did to Bonhoeffer what Herod had done to Christ—he went after him. Bonhoeffer was placed in a concentration camp, where he died for what he believed.[8] Bonhoeffer believed Jesus when he said, "Do not be afraid of those who kill the body but cannot kill the soul" (Matthew 10:28 NIV).

Do you have a dangerous faith, one that isn't afraid to follow the mission that is laid out before you no matter the cost or where it may take you?

Is God calling to you leave your comfort zone and invite a neighbor to church or to a Bible study? Is God calling you to take a leap of faith and give sacrificially to your church in order to grow its outreach to your community? Is God calling you to trust in the gifts he has given you to be a voice of hope and faith in your local schools, your community, or your home? Is God calling you to stand above the culture and raise your voice against an injustice like human trafficking? Is God calling you to come face-to-face with the need in your area: to minister to those who are homeless, to open your heart and home to a child in the foster care system, or to mentor a youth who doesn't have a father? Is God calling you to face the unknown and offer yourself as a light into the world on a mission trip to Guatemala, India, or China? Following a mighty God like ours can be dangerous.

At Christmastime, we often gather around to gaze at peaceful scenes of Jesus as a baby, lying in a manger, surrounded by the familiar characters of the Christmas story. He is precious, tiny, and divine. But we know that the story doesn't stop there. Jesus came to do a dangerous work in the world—to destroy the power of death and sin and restore us into a right relationship with himself. His message is not safe; his love for us is undaunted. He was not afraid to walk into the dark crevices of this world with his light. "For God so loved the world"—for God so loved *us*—"that he gave his one and only Son, that whoever believes in him shall not perish but have eternal life" (John 3:16 NIV). He fights for our hearts with his extraordinary love, and his sacrifice leads our hearts to say, "Yes, Lord, we will follow."

Reflect

The birth of Jesus sent shockwaves through the world and the celestial realms. How does reflecting on Jesus' dangerous mission impact your view of Christmas—the celebration of his birth?

_____

_____

_____

_____

_____

What is your response to the "danger" of the gospel?

_____

_____

_____

_____

_____

Meditate

"Do not suppose that I have come to bring peace to the earth; I did not come to bring peace, but a sword. For I have come to turn

"'a man against his father,
  and a daughter against her mother,
and a daughter-in-law against her mother-in-law;
  a man's enemies will be the members of his own household.'"

Matthew 10:34-36 NIV

Finally, be strong in the Lord and in his mighty power. Put on the full armor of God, so that you can take your stand against the devil's schemes. For our struggle is not against flesh and blood, but against the rulers, against the authorities, against the powers of this dark world and against the spiritual forces of evil in the heavenly realms.

Ephesians 6:10-12 NIV

"My prayer is not that you take them out of the world but that you protect them from the evil one. They are not of the world, even as I am not of it. Sanctify them by the truth; your word is truth. As you sent me into the world, I have sent them into the world. For them I sanctify myself, that they too may be truly sanctified."

John 17:14-19 NIV

Pray

Heavenly Father, do a dangerous work in my heart this Christmas. Shatter my expectations and lead me into places where I can only rely on you. Help me to trust in your goodness and love for me. Thank you for sending your Son to shatter the bonds of sin and open the door to you. Help me accept the love and forgiveness that you so boldly and freely offer as you take me by the hand and go to work in my life. Amen.

3.
God Is Jealous

3.
God Is Jealous

Andy Nixon

"'Love the Lord your God with all your heart and with all your soul and with all your strength and with all your mind'; and, 'Love your neighbor as yourself.'"

Luke 10:27 NIV

There's nothing like witnessing the look of pure joy on a child's face as he or she unwraps gifts on Christmas morning. We parents stand by and watch, cameras rolling, as the gasps and giggles and shrieks begin; and before you can blink twice, the mountain of beautifully wrapped presents is reduced to the rubble of shredded paper and debris littering the carpet.

Let's face it—in our society, Christmas has largely become all about the gifts. And though gift-gifting traditions are fun to celebrate with the ones we love, each year at Christmas, as gifts pile up under the tree, I am convicted anew of the selfishness of the human heart. It's not that we are more selfish or greedy this time of the year, it's just that Christmastime seems to heighten those impulses, and we give a lot of time and energy to the effort. Lists are made and money is spent. We start wishing and hoping and dreaming of getting that perfect gift we've always wanted, and we dream about how excited our children will be when we give them the new gadget they've been begging for all year.

The whole gift-giving process can be so consuming, our greed so over-powering, our minds in such overdrive that we end up simply giving lip service to the thing we're really supposed to be celebrating—the birth of Jesus, our Savior. And I have to wonder, *Does that make God jealous?*

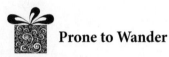 **Prone to Wander**

Jealous is not how we often think of our holy God. We tend to use the word *jealous* to communicate pettiness or envy. We are jealous of our colleague for receiving a promotion; we are envious of our neighbor's new sports car in the driveway. Yet, on several occasions, "jealous" is how the Old Testament describes God:

> *Do not worship any other god, for the* LORD, *whose name is Jealous, is a jealous God.*
>
> Exodus 34:14 NIV

> *For the* LORD *your God is a consuming fire, a jealous God.*
>
> Deuteronomy 4:24 NIV

> *Fear the* LORD *your God, serve him only and take your oaths in his name. Do not follow other gods, the gods of peoples around you; for the* LORD *your God, who is among you, is a jealous God and his anger will burn against you, and he will destroy you from the face of the land.*
>
> Deuteronomy 6:13-15 NIV

Yikes! Sounds pretty intense, right? So what is the Old Testament trying to tell us by using *jealous* as a description—even a name—for God?

The Hebrew word for *jealousy* is *qin'ah*, which means "warmth" or "heat," and it is used to describe intense emotion and passion.[1] When Scripture uses this word for God, it is describing how God is intensely passionate about his people—you might say he is "on fire" for us—and how God's love for us causes him to be jealous of anything that stands between us and him—namely, our idols.

As the Old Testament repeatedly illustrates, God's people often get their priorities out of order and are easily distracted by their own desires. In Exodus 32, we read about how God has rescued the people of Israel out of slavery in Egypt and is leading them toward the Promised Land. Moses, their leader, leaves the group to go up onto the mountain in order to receive instructions from the Lord. He is gone for longer than the people expect, and so they begin to panic. They start to wonder if they've been abandoned, if God really is looking out for them. They decide they need to take matters into their own hands, and so they create an idol to worship in place of the Lord. You could say that made God a little hot under the collar.

Then the Lord said to Moses, "Go down, because your people, whom you brought up out of Egypt, have become corrupt. They have been quick to turn away from what I commanded them and have made themselves an idol cast in the shape of a calf. They have bowed down to it and sacrificed to it and have said, 'These are your gods, Israel, who brought you up out of Egypt.'

"I have seen these people," the Lord said to Moses, "and they are a stiff-necked people. Now leave me alone so that my anger may burn against them and that I may destroy them. Then I will make you into a great nation."

But Moses sought the favor of the Lord his God. "Lord," he said, "why should your anger burn against your people, whom you brought out of Egypt with great power and a mighty hand? Why should the Egyptians say, 'It was with evil intent that he brought them out, to kill them in the mountains and to wipe them off the face of the earth'? Turn from your fierce anger; relent and do not bring disaster on your people. Remember your servants Abraham, Isaac and Israel, to whom you swore by your own self: 'I will make your descendants as numerous as the stars in the sky and I will give your descendants all this land I promised them, and it will be their inheritance forever.'" Then the LORD relented and did not bring on his people the disaster he had threatened.

Exodus 32:7-14 NIV

God had rescued his people from slavery and set them on the path to freedom because he loved them and wanted to have a relationship with them. God's passion for their freedom caused him to be jealous of anything that stood in the way of that freedom. And that is how he feels about us. God is passionate about us, and when God's passion for us cannot be fully expressed because of idolatrous choices we have made, he gets—in a word—*jealous*.

Does this make God some kind of vengeful, wronged lover who is out to get us when our eyes (or hearts) wander? Not at all. The reason God wants us to keep our eyes on him is because he knows that our idols can destroy us and keep us from experiencing the life-giving freedom he offers. In John 10:10 Jesus proclaims, "The thief comes only to steal and kill and destroy; I have come that they may have life, and have it to the full" (NIV).

God, our Creator, is eager for us to live in his fullness, and the only way that will happen is if we put God and our relationship with him first in our hearts. Our idolatry also has a way of distracting us from God's plans and pulling us off course. Right before the people of Israel are about to enter the Promised Land, Moses gives them these last-minute instructions: "Do not worship any other god, for the LORD, whose name is Jealous, is a jealous God" (Exodus 34:14 NIV). Jealous is God's name. Moses' warning reminds me of the last-minute wisdom I try to impart to my fourteen-year-old son every morning as he runs out the door: "Remember to turn in your homework! Be nice! Work hard!" At a pivotal time in the life of Israel, Moses is reminding the people of their priorities and urging them to keep God first in their lives.

Putting God First

God makes no apologies about wanting to have first place in our lives, and his jealousy for our hearts is revealed in his sending Jesus to us. Through Jesus, we see just how jealous God is for a relationship with us—and how committed he was to getting it. In no better place does the gospel express this idea than in John 3:16, a verse worth repeating: "For God so loved the world that he gave his one and only Son, that whoever believes in him shall not perish but have eternal life" (NIV).

God didn't send just another messenger—not another Moses, not another prophet—to show us his love for us; instead, he sent his one and only Son to come and live with us so that we could intimately know his heart and live in community with him. Through Jesus, we see just how jealous God is for us. We see how much God wants to know us and how much he wants to be known by us. Jesus was the Word made flesh, God living among us (see John 1:14). God sent Jesus to say, "This is me! I want you to know me." When we know Jesus and the love he has for us, it changes our lives and, through us, it changes the world.

The season of Advent serves as a great reminder of how much God loves us and how he moved heaven and earth on that first Christmas Day in order to be in relationship with us. As we prepare to celebrate Jesus' coming to earth, it is important for us to examine our hearts. Just as the Israelites were reminded of God's jealousy before he made a big move in their lives, Advent can serve as a reminder for us that God is moving in our hearts and lives and is jealous for first place in our hearts.

So, practically speaking, what does putting God first in our lives look like? It means we spend time reading the Bible, God's Word, and asking him to speak to us through it. It means we are people of prayer—that we are in an ongoing conversation with God about our needs and desires, and that we use our time in prayer to listen for God's voice. It means we, as people who have been set free by the love of Jesus, commit ourselves to generosity and serving other people in order to share his life-giving love with them.

It means we ask ourselves the question, *Am I available for Jesus to work in me?* This is a dangerous question but a necessary one. It's important to take time to look inside our hearts and ask ourselves if we really are willing to follow God wherever he leads, if we are willing to drop our own plans to follow his.

Jesus taught us that making God our first and only love would be essential to following him. When asked what the most important commandment was, Jesus answered, "'Love the Lord your God with all your heart and with all your soul and with all your strength and with all your mind'; and, 'Love your neighbor as yourself'" (Luke 10:27 NIV).

When we place God first in our hearts, we make ourselves available for God to move in and through us. I was reminded of this about a year ago as I began to sense God calling me to be more available to those in my congregation and community. As I prayed each morning, I felt God asking me to open my heart and my life to the people around me. Through Scripture he reminded me how Jesus made himself accessible to those who wanted to learn from him and was very public in his approach to teaching and ministering (see Matthew 26:55).

While I was pondering where God was leading me in this area, I began reading the book *Love Does* by Bob Goff, which encourages believers to put the love of God into action. Bob believes in connecting with and encouraging others so much that, at the end of the book, he gives out his personal cell phone number and invites anyone to call him. *Seriously? This guy is crazy!* I thought. I couldn't believe he would be so open and available to anyone who wanted to give him a call. Then I began to put some things together. I remembered my prayer time and how God had reminded me how open Jesus was. I thought of how the great preacher John Wesley spoke of Jesus wherever he was, whether in a pulpit, a field, or a cemetery. I wondered, *How open is my heart to where the Holy Spirit is leading?*

So I made the decision to give out my cell phone number to the members of my congregation and anyone else who wanted it. We even printed little magnets with the number on it that we give away to church visitors and new members. Granted, it's a little weird when I'm in the gas station restroom and see my number stuck to the wall, but living for Jesus has its risks, I guess.

I followed God's lead to give out my number because I want my love for Jesus and for people to come first. I want to be open to where God leads, and I want to be accessible to anyone who has questions and wants to know more about God. As a result, I've seen God do some pretty wonderful things. I've seen firsthand how, when we are willing to ask God to become number one in our hearts and to make ourselves available to what he wants to do through us, God begins to move and spread his love to the corners of the world.

 ## Love in Action

As we begin to open ourselves to the plans God has for us, he never hesitates to do really great things through our willingness.

There is a tradition in our house that on the opening night of football season we get some buffalo wings and gather around the TV to watch the game. This year's opening game was no different. I ordered wings online from my usual haunt; and when I got there to pick them up, I saw there was an unusually long line at the counter.

It is a small place, and the guy behind the counter was the only employee. Every time I've been there, this guy has been amazing at customer service. He is polite, thorough, and asks about my day. He gets the order right every time and always has a great smile on his face. But on this visit, I could tell he was stressed. He was flinging bowls and slamming doors. He was under pressure, and it showed. Finally he snapped. He just stopped what he was doing, looked at all of us who were waiting, and said, "I make fifty-four dollars a day after taxes. Fifty-four dollars a day. Which one of you wants to come back here and do this job for that?"

Silence from the crowd. It was awkward. Highly awkward. I glanced at the cars outside the window, and it was pretty safe to assume that all of us in there made more than fifty-four dollars a day.

"Which one of you is Andy?" he asked.

Oh no, not good, I thought. Reluctantly, I stepped up.

"You ordered online," he said. "You've paid, and your wings are in the bag on the counter. You can take them and go."

Relieved, I did just that. But on the way home, Jesus began to work on my heart.

"What are you going to do about that whole situation?" he asked.

"Me? Nothing. I'm off-duty."

Jesus asked again. "How many times have you thought of complimenting him or telling his supervisor how well he does his job?"

Truthfully, I had thought about doing so dozens of times, but I had never followed through with my good intentions. So when I got home, I sent a complimentary note to his supervisor through the company website, clicked send, and got ready to enjoy my wings. But Jesus didn't let me off that easily.

"If you really loved him, you'd do more, Andy."

Jesus was right. So the next day I called the wing place, found out when he was scheduled to work next, and made a plan. I told the story on social media and asked my friends, "Would you love on this guy?" I posted the date, time, and location, and I asked my friends to put a love flash mob into action. "Go by and tell him 'I am praying for you' or just say 'hi'—whatever comes to mind," I suggested.

And they did. On that day many people dropped by to say "hi" or tell him that they were praying for him. Someone brought him cupcakes. One person took him balloons and another a grocery store gift card. At the end of the night, a church member went in with his son to eat wings. "How was your day?" he asked the worker.

"It has been amazing," he said. "Business is good, and I got cupcakes and balloons—all because a pastor told a story. It has been unbelievable! I'd love to thank him."

The church member asked, "Do you want his number?"

He called me. We talked. He asked me to pray for him, his wife, and his kids. I did (and still do). The next time I went into the restaurant I introduced myself, and he came out from behind the counter and gave me a big hug. I still get a hug every time I go in there.

The Holy Spirit speaks to each and every one of us, and how we choose to respond is important. That experience made me realize that God had a plan, and he wanted to make it happen through me. God was jealous for me to stop what I was doing and to put his love into action, to show his love to someone else in a small way that made a huge difference in his heart and in my own. I learned that when we put God's plans ahead of our own—when we say "yes" to God—he will move, and amazing things will happen.

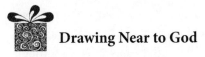 **Drawing Near to God**

When we put Jesus first in our hearts—when we give him the priority and time he deserves—only then can we truly know him and his heart for us.

Recently my wife recognized that we were a little disconnected from each other because of our busyness and all the distractions life throws our way. She sensed it and took action. She bought a giant jigsaw puzzle—a 1,500-piece fall scene with acres and acres of pumpkins and barns in varying shades of orange that almost numbed the mind.

"We are going to do this puzzle together," she said.

Oh no, I thought. *Here we go.* So for weeks, on the evenings we were home we worked this puzzle together. We worked on this puzzle for what felt like so long I could see it when I closed my eyes. One night we were talking while working the puzzle, sharing our thoughts and dreams and talking about the kids and our jobs.

"Do you feel more connected to me?" she asked. "Is our relationship better because of this time together?"

You know what? It was. I didn't see it at first, but something as simple as spending a little dedicated, focused time with my wife not only strengthened my marriage but also served as a reminder that I need to make time with the one I love in order to keep our relationship strong and healthy.

It's the same in our relationship with God. Spending time in the Bible, in prayer, in worship, and in serving others are ways that deepen our relationship with Jesus. When we put Jesus first in our time and efforts, we learn more about him and his heart for us and others. This opens us to where he is leading, making us free to show others his love and goodness.

The season of Advent is all about preparation—not preparing our trees or our houses or our presents or our lists, but preparing our hearts for God to do a great work. It is a time to take a look into our hearts and ask, *What is number one in my heart?* God is jealous for that spot. He loves us so much that he wants us to experience the power his love has to change our hearts and the lives of those around us. He wants to us to do amazing things. But more than that, he wants us to know him intimately and to be able to let go of our plans and freely experience the glorious gift he has given us through Jesus Christ:

You can be sure that God will take care of everything you need, his generosity exceeding even yours in the glory that pours from Jesus. Our God and Father abounds in glory that just pours out into eternity. Yes.
Philippians 4:19-20 THE MESSAGE

This Christmas, can you revel in God's lavish jealousy for you? Will you trust in his great love and dare to believe that his plans for you are greater than anything you can imagine? You see, God's plans are always best; his passionate love for you is perfect and complete. God wants you to experience the fullness of his love and then put that love into action.

This Christmas, will you put him first? Will you open your heart and your life to his leading?

Reflect

How does it make you feel to know that God is jealous for your heart? Have you ever considered that before? Do you feel God speaking to you about any areas where you might have put something or someone ahead of him?

_____

_____

_____

_____

_____

How could putting God in first place this Advent change you? How could it change your family and the way that you celebrate the season together?

_____

_____

_____

_____

Meditate

"Therefore I tell you, do not worry about your life, what you will eat or drink; or about your body, what you will wear. Is not life more than food, and the body more than clothes? Look at the birds of the air; they do not sow or reap or store away in barns, and yet your heavenly Father feeds them. Are you not much more valuable than they? Can any one of you by worrying add a single hour to your life?

"And why do you worry about clothes? See how the flowers of the field grow. They do not labor or spin. Yet I tell you that not even Solomon in all his splendor was dressed like one of these. If that is how God clothes the grass of the field, which is here today and tomorrow is thrown into the fire, will he not much more clothe you—you of little faith? So do not worry, saying, 'What shall we eat?' or 'What shall we drink?' or 'What shall we wear?' For the pagans run after all these things, and your heavenly Father knows that you need them. But seek first his kingdom and his righteousness, and all these things will be given to you as well."

Matthew 6:25-33 NIV

*"No eye has seen, no ear has heard,
    and no mind has imagined
what God has prepared
    for those who love him."*

1 Corinthians 2:9 NLT

Therefore, I urge you, brothers and sisters, in view of God's mercy, to offer your bodies as a living sacrifice, holy and pleasing to God—this is your true and proper worship. Do not conform to the pattern of this world, but be transformed by the renewing of your mind. Then you will be able to test and approve what God's will is—his good, pleasing and perfect will.

Romans 12:1-2 NIV

Therefore, since we are surrounded by such a great cloud of witnesses, let us throw off everything that hinders and the sin that so easily entangles. And let us run with perseverance the race marked out for us, fixing our eyes on Jesus, the pioneer and perfecter of faith. For the joy set before him he endured the cross, scorning its shame, and sat down at the right hand of the throne of God. Consider him who endured such opposition from sinners, so that you will not grow weary and lose heart.

Hebrews 12:1-3 NIV

Pray

Heavenly Father, thank you for fighting for our hearts—for my heart. I confess that I easily wander away from you and give my heart to things and people. I confess that I often love myself more than I love you. Forgive me and draw me close to you. Help me to understand the power of your love for me, and teach me how to show your love to others. Be first in my heart, Lord. Make me ready to receive all that you want to do in and through me. Amen.

4.
God Is Faithful

4.
God Is Faithful

Rob Renfroe

This is what the Lord says:

"In the time of my favor I will answer you,
*   and in the day of salvation I will help you;*
I will keep you and will make you
*   to be a covenant for the people,*
to restore the land
*   and to reassign its desolate inheritances,*
to say to the captives, 'Come out,'
*   and to those in darkness, 'Be free!'"*

"They will feed beside the roads
*   and find pasture on every barren hill.*
They will neither hunger nor thirst,
*   nor will the desert heat or the sun beat down on them.*
He who has compassion on them will guide them
*   and lead them beside springs of water. . . ."*

Shout for joy, you heavens;
rejoice, you earth;
burst into song, you mountains!
*For the L*ord *comforts his people*
and will have compassion on his afflicted ones. . . .

"Can a mother forget the baby at her breast
and have no compassion on the child she has borne?
Though she may forget,
I will not forget you!
See, I have engraved you on the palms of my hands.
                                    Isaiah 49:8-10, 13, 15-16a NIV

It's painful to be forgotten or left behind, especially by someone who has promised to be there for you. A trusted friend stops returning your calls, and what you thought was a life-giving friendship now doesn't seem to matter to your friend at all. Your boss assures you, "We are all family in this company," but then the economy goes south, you have a bad quarter, and you hear the words, "I'm sorry to have to let you go; it's not personal—it's just business." Your spouse betrays you or rejects you, and you wonder if all those vows and promises you made so long ago ever meant anything at all.

The pain we suffer in moments such as these can be excruciating. When someone we trust—someone we love and thought loved us—walks away or lets us down, it makes us wonder, *Can I really count on anyone? And if I can't trust the people who promised to be there for me, maybe I really am all alone in this world.* Times like these can make us feel lost and alone—perhaps even wondering where God is in the midst of our pain and broken relationships.

In these moments—and in the midst of life's many challenges—we need to be reminded of who God is and what he has done for us. The season of Advent is a time when we stop and remember these truths. We pause in the middle of our busy lives; we sit in the midst of all of our hopes and longings; we pray and meditate. We ask hard questions, and we look to the

Word of God to be reminded that he is a God of faithfulness and one who keeps his promises, no matter the cost.

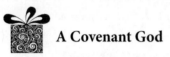 A Covenant God

The whole story of the Bible tells us that God is faithful and serious about the promise—the covenant—that he has made to be with his people. Scripture tells us of this covenant in a powerful story that begins in Genesis 15 with a man called Abram.

God calls Abram to leave his homeland and his family, not knowing where he is going, and to trust God for the future. God makes a covenant with Abram, promising that he will give Abram a land to dwell in, that he will grant Abram many descendants, and that he will be their God. God promises to bless Abram's family and bring blessing to the world through their lineage.

Covenant is a word that's used often in the Bible, but it is a word that is never used lightly. It is reserved for formal agreements of a most serious nature involving elaborate oaths and vows that must be taken to enter into the agreement. When I officiate a wedding, I like to remind the couple that they are at the altar making a covenant with one another, not agreeing to a contract. There is a huge difference between the two. A contract says, "If you do something for me, I will do something for you; but if you fail to live up to your part of the bargain, I no longer have to fulfill my part of the deal."

A covenant—at least the way the Bible often uses the term—is altogether different. It is a commitment to fulfill an oath, even if the other person fails in his or her commitment. In many areas of life, contracts are preferable to covenants. For instance, when you arrange for a contractor to build a house for you, you don't want a covenant, which says that regardless of whether the contractor builds the house on time or according to spec— or even builds it at all—you pledge to pay the contractor the full amount by a particular day. Not a chance!

When you're building a house, you want a contract that says if they don't build, then you don't pay. But when you're building a home, a marriage, you want a covenant. You don't want a contract marriage that says: "If you love me, then I'll love you back. I will love you as long as you are easy to love. I will love you as long as you are pleasing to me. I will love you as long as you make me happy." You want a covenant marriage that says: "I will love, honor, and cherish you, for better for worse, for richer for poorer, in sickness and in health, until death do us part."

If you see your marriage as a contract, the question is always, "Am I getting what I was promised?" But when you see your marriage as a covenant, the question becomes, "Am *I* giving what *I* promised?" A contract marriage asks, "Is my wife or husband living up to the vows she or he took?" But a covenant marriage asks, "Am *I* living up to the vows *I* took? Am I providing all that I promised to love, honor, cherish, and treasure this person?" Contract marriages can work for a time. They can bring happiness for a season. They can be endured forever. But covenant marriages find a way to love and serve through the difficult times. The hardships of life do not break the covenant but make it stronger. It's only when a marriage is a covenant that two people grow and mature together—that two people truly become one.

In Genesis 15 God says, "Abram, I make a covenant with you. I will bless you and your descendants, I will give you a land, I will be your God, and I will do something through your descendants that will bring blessing to all the world." And Abram says to God, "But God, I don't even have a real descendant, and already I'm an old man. How can I know that you will keep your promise? How can I know that you will be faithful to the covenant that you're making with me today?" So God instructs Abram to bring a heifer, a goat, and a ram; cut them in half; and separate the halves with a space in between. Abram obeys, and a strange thing happens.

> *As the sun was setting, Abram fell into a deep sleep. . . . When the sun had set and darkness had fallen, a smoking firepot with a blazing torch appeared and passed between the pieces. On that day the LORD made a covenant with Abram. . .*
>
> Genesis 15:12, 17-18 NIV

What's going on here? We are told that God was making a covenant with Abram; and at this time in history, when two parties joined together in a covenant, an elaborate ritual was held. Animals would be sacrificed and their carcasses divided, and the parties making the covenant would walk between the divided carcasses—as the Lord does on this night. Abram would have understood that the meaning behind this action was this: "May what has been done to these animals be done to me if I fail to keep the covenant I have made with you." Abram had asked God, "How can I be certain you will keep your covenant? How can I know you will honor your promises? How can I be sure and base my entire life on the belief that you will be faithful to your word?" And to answer Abram's questions, the presence of God—symbolized by a burning torch—passed between the carcasses, God affirming, "I would rather die than be unfaithful to the promise I make to you today."

Our God is not a contract God. Our God is not an "I will love you as long as you make me happy" kind of God. He's not an "I will love you as long as you do everything right" kind of God or an "I will love you as long as you don't fail me" kind of God. That's not our God. Our God is not a contract God.

Our God is a covenant God. Our God is a God who says, "I will remain true even if you are false. I will remain faithful even if you are unfaithful. I will continue to love you even if you don't love me back." Our God is a for-better-or-for-worse kind of God. And his promise to Abram is the same promise he gives to us: "I will love you and I will be faithful to you, even if it kills me."

 An Unlikely Love Story

Unfortunately, God's people are often quick to test his faithfulness. In fact, the whole story of the Old Testament is basically one of a faithful God and an unfaithful people. God sends Moses to Egypt to bring the Israelites out of slavery, and they have barely gotten into the wilderness before they begin to complain and grumble: "We should just go back to Egypt. It's too hard out here following God. We want to go back to slavery. At least there we had meat to eat!" Almost no time passes before they create a golden calf and bow down and worship a god of their own making rather than the God who saved them.

Forty years later, when God finally brings the Israelites into the Promised Land, a land of prosperity, they again forget his graciousness and turn to the gods of that land. When enemies attack, God raises up deliverers such as Gideon and Deborah who defend them. When they are taken away into exile, overtaken by foreign armies and powerful kings, God miraculously works, remembering his covenant and bringing his people back to the land that he had promised them. Throughout all of this, and over hundreds of years and many generations, God sends prophets to speak his words so the people know his mind. Some prophets God sends to chastise and convict them of their idolatry and their sins; others he sends to comfort and assure them of his love.

The prophet Isaiah, mourning the people's unfaithfulness, writes, "I will sing for the one I love / a song about his vineyard: / My loved one had a vineyard / on a fertile hillside. / He dug it up and cleared it of stones / and planted it with the choicest vines. / He built a watchtower in it / and cut out a wine press as well. / Then he looked for a crop of good grapes, / but it yielded only bad fruit" (5:1-2 NIV). Then, in the next two verses, God himself speaks: "Now you dwellers in Jerusalem and people of Judah, / judge between me and my vineyard. / What more could have been done for my vineyard / than I have done for it? / When I look for good grapes / why did it yield only bad?" (vv. 3-4 NIV).

When the people of Israel begin wondering, *Has God forgotten us? Has he forsaken us?* God reassures them,

Can a mother forget the baby at her breast / and have no compassion on the child she has borne? / Though she may forget, / I will not forget you! / See, I have engraved you on the palms of my hands.

Isaiah 49:15-16a NIV

Think about that for a moment. If you are a parent, what would have to happen for you to walk away and forget the child that you love more than life, the child you once carried in your body, the child you dreamed of and prayed for before he or she was born, the child you rocked to sleep at night and cared for when he or she was sick? What would your child have to do for you to walk away and say, "I forget you; I no longer care"? In this passage, God says to the Israelites, and to every one of us, "Should you act in such a way that even your own mother or father turns from you—should you exhaust those who love you most—even then, I will not forsake you. I will not forget you. There is nothing you can do to make me run away. I will be faithful to you."

The story of the Old Testament is consistent; it is the love story of a faithful God and an unfaithful people. It would have been so easy for God to say, "Enough! I've given you all that I can give. I've loved you as long as I can love you. I've reached out to you as long as I can. Enough is enough, and now I walk away." It would have been easy for God to do that if he were a contract God. But our God is a covenant God. Our God is a God who says, "I will not forget my love for you, no matter what you do. Even though you walk away from me, I will remain true and faithful."

 ## A Bigger Story

We celebrate that Christmas is about a baby and a young mother and shepherds and wise men. But God has always known that Christmas is about something bigger. Christmas is about keeping a promise. Christmas is about being faithful.

There are many benefits of Jesus coming into our world—all of them important. We needed to know more about God and how he wants us to live. But if that was the only reason for Christmas, Jesus could have come as a teacher and nothing more. We needed God's healing power to bind up our broken places and heal our physical and emotional wounds. But if that had been the only reason for Christmas, Jesus could have come as a healer and nothing more. We needed God's help to get along with one another and strengthen our relationships. But if that was the only reason for Christmas, Jesus could have come as a counselor and nothing more. We needed God's help to help make the world a fairer and more just place. But if that was the only reason for Christmas, Jesus could have come as a prophet and nothing more.

But the problem goes deeper than that; we needed something more. When the angel appeared to Joseph to announce that Mary would have a child, he said, "She will give birth to a son, and you are to give him the name Jesus, because he will save his people from their sins" (Matthew 1:21 NIV). The name Jesus has significant meaning; it is Hebrew for "the Lord saves."[1] So when the angel proclaimed the news of Jesus' birth to the shepherds, he said, "Do not be afraid. I bring you good news that will cause great joy for all the people. Today in the town of David a Savior has been born to you; he is the Messiah, the Lord" (Luke 2:10-11 NIV).

The baby born that day was not a teacher, a healer, a counselor, or a prophet. Yes, Jesus was all of those things. But when the angel had to pick one title—the most important one, the one that would give us God's *why* for Christmas—he said, "A *Savior* has been born to you."

Jesus was born to be a Savior, and Christmas was God's plan to bring him into the world. Why? Because we desperately need a Savior. We can't do it on our own, so God made a way to fulfill his covenant to us. You see, when we were lost in our sins, when we had rebelled against God's love, when we had rejected his mercy and his kindness, he became incarnate in the person of Jesus Christ so that he could show us the depths of his love and faithfulness. Instead of walking away from us, he walked into our world to bear our griefs and sorrows and pay the penalty of our sins so that we might be forgiven and made right with the God who is faithful even when we are not.

The good news of great joy that comes to us on Christmas Day is that God has made a way, and the way is Jesus. The way is a Savior who would take our place, suffer our punishment, and make atonement for our sins.

I need a Savior. You need a Savior. Joseph and Mary and the shepherds and the wise men needed a Savior. That is the *why* of Christmas— God's plan from the beginning. Christmas was always about a cross.

The Price of God's Faithfulness

We Christians have the most interesting concept of God. We describe God as one in three persons; we refer to this concept as the Trinity. It's hard to understand or explain, but we came to hold this doctrine because Jesus spoke of God in heaven when he was on earth, one he referred to as the Father. Jesus also said, "I and the Father are one" (John 10:30 NIV), and he claimed all the rights of deity for himself—the right to forgive sins (see Matthew 9:1-8), to judge the world (see Matthew 25:31-46), and even to be worshiped (see John 20:24-29). Then he spoke of the Spirit of God coming upon his people when he returned to heaven (see John 14:15-17). It's a difficult concept, and no one fully understands it. But we surely know that the relationship between God the Father and Jesus the Son is at least as deep and caring as the relationship that a loving earthly father has with his own son (or daughter). And so, in order to keep his promise of faithfulness to his people, God the Son became incarnate on Christmas Day, knowing that he would be mocked and rejected, scourged, spit upon, and crucified. And to keep his promise, God the Father knew he would have to allow it to happen to the one he loved.

Years ago when the movie *The Passion of the Christ* first arrived in theaters, I hesitated to go see it. I must have been asked a hundred times, "What did you think about *The Passion of the Christ*? . . . You haven't seen it? Well, you're going to see it, aren't you?"

I'd tell people, "I don't know. . . . I don't really want to see it."

And they'd respond: "But why? It's about Jesus!"

Exactly. It's about the one I love—the one I owe my life to—and I know what's going to happen. The one I love is going to be beaten and mistreated. A crown of thorns is going to be forced into his forehead, and spikes are going to be nailed into his hands and feet. And evil men are going to stand around his bruised and bloodied body, laughing at him and calling him a fool.

I have read the story many, many times, and I knew it would be painful and devastating to have a visual experience of what they did to him.

I was afraid it would seem too real, and I couldn't help but wonder, *What if it was my son who was suffering in that way?* What if I had to stand by and hear what they were saying about my child—naming him a fool, calling him cursed, and laughing at his shame? And what if I saw the nails and the blood and knew that my son—my joy—had harmed no one and done no wrong but only loved. Then, in his lowest moment, as he saw the dark shadow fall near and felt the breath of death upon his neck, he was utterly alone. His friends were gone. His disciples had left. And he thought I too had forgotten him. If I had the power, could I have stayed my hand, remained silent, and refused to save his life? And for what? To honor a promise, to keep a commitment, to be faithful to a man named Abram and his descendants who had been so unfaithful? To reach out to a lost and ugly world to whom I had said, "I will be faithful. I will love you even if it kills me"?

In one of Russian author Fyodor Dostoyevsky's novels, he describes a man who stares at a large painting of Jesus' broken body and is mesmerized by it. It's as if he melds into the painting—as though he's in the middle of it, looking around. And the horror of what happened there on the cross seeps into the man's heart and mind. He sees the physical suffering that Jesus went through, and he begins to understand the emotional shame of being crucified, of being laughed at and mocked. As he realizes the spiritual agony of Jesus' darkest moment, it grips his heart and he says, "A man could even lose his faith from that painting."[2] In other words, who wants to worship a God who doesn't seem to love his Son any more than this? Why would God seemingly allow evil to win?

 Because He First Loved Us

My friend Tommy was kind of a rough and rugged guy. He was a member of a church that I once served, but he wasn't like our typical members. Most of our members were professionals—bankers and doctors and lawyers and dentists. But Tommy was different—he was a farmer, a blue jeans and T-shirt kind of guy. He'd had a very rough-and-tumble life, but somewhere along the way Jesus Christ had become real to him; and when he trusted in Christ, his heart was changed. He was a good husband and a good father. He was a good friend and a good church member.

I'll never forget the night I got a phone call saying that his daughter, Suzy, had been in a terrible wreck and had been taken to a nearby hospital. When I got there, I found her on life support. After a week, the decision was made to let her go. I had seen the family at the hospital and had prayed with them, but I dreaded this last visit. What would I say? How could I help them process what had happened? We prayed in a private waiting room before they went in to see Suzy for the last time. As we opened our eyes, Tommy looked up at me and said, "Rob, there's something I can't figure out."

Here it comes, I thought, the question I've dreaded, the question pastors often face in these kinds of situations and the one that none of us have the answer to: *Why?*

"I'm about to go in there and let my daughter die," Tommy said. "It's the hardest thing I've ever had to do. Just thinking about it rips my heart out. I wouldn't do it if there was any other way. And what I've been wrestling with is this: God did the very same thing with Jesus. He let his Son die because he loved me. I just can't figure out why he would love me the way he does."

Why would Jesus come, knowing that he would die an awful death? And why would the Father let his Son die in pain and shame? I can give you the answer, though it's difficult to fully comprehend. Here it is: Because God loves you.

Because God is faithful to you and to his promises.

Because God gave us laws to keep us pure and close to him, but the laws did not change our hearts.

Because God sent his prophets to turn us away from our sin, but the words of the prophets did not change our hearts.

And so God the Son came to earth, and God the Father allowed him to do so.

Jesus came into this world to bear our sorrows, our griefs, and our sins; he came to die for us and pay a price that we could not pay. We could not redeem ourselves; we could not break the hardness of our own hearts and clean up our own sin. And so he came in the person of Jesus to die in our place, knowing that if he kept his word, if he fulfilled his promise to love us even if it meant his life, then that kind of love and faithfulness would make it possible for us to dwell fully with him.

Our God is a faithful God. He gave us his own Son. He suffered incredible, unimaginable pain so that we would know that he loves us, so that we could be made right and our sins could be forgiven. Friend, God's message in Jesus from the cradle to the cross is not that God did not love his Son but that God loves *you*. The reason that he came, which we celebrate on Christmas Day, and the reason that he died on the cross is that he is faithful to *you*—he is faithful to the promises that he has made. He was faithful to his covenant to bring blessing to the world through the heirs of Abraham.

So on Christmas Day we celebrate that God the Son became incarnate, coming into our world while knowing the price that he would have to pay to redeem us from our sin. And God the Father allowed him to do it *for you*.

You can trust God. You can trust every promise that God has made to you because God has already proven he is faithful. He said, "The one who comes to Me I will by no means cast out" (John 6:37 NKJV). If you have wandered away from God and wonder if you can come back home, know that God is faithful. He will not cast you away. If you've done things that you're ashamed of and don't want to admit them to yourself, much less to God, he has promised, "I will forgive your sins and remember them no more" (see Hebrews 8:12). You can come and put them at the foot of the cross. He will forgive you. He has promised, and he is faithful.

The beautiful truth of the gospel—and of Christmas—is that you are not alone. At the heart of the universe is a heart that is faithful and true. And the one who possesses that heart says, "I promise." He says,

I will forgive your sins and remember your transgressions no more (Psalm 103:12).

I will never leave you or forsake you (Hebrews 13:5).

I will send my Spirit to bring you comfort and power and wisdom (John 14:18).

I will provide for all your needs (Philippians 4:19).

You can trust our God because he is a covenant God. Our God is a for-better-or-for-worse kind of God. Our God is a till-death-do-us-part kind of God—and even *then* he's an I'm-not-through-loving-you kind of God. He will not forget you. How could he? Your name is engraved on the palms of his hands.

Our God is forever and always faithful.

Reflect

As a descendant of Abram, how does it make you feel to know that the God of the universe has made such a complete and full promise to be faithful to you, no matter what?

_____

_____

_____

_____

_____

Consider how God's faithfulness came to full fruition through the cross. How might remembering this truth change the way you celebrate the birth of our Savior, Jesus, this Christmas?

_____

_____

_____

_____

_____

Meditate

God, speaking of Jesus, says: *"I, the LORD, have called you in righteousness; / I will take hold of your hand. / I will keep you and will make you / to be a covenant for the people / and a light for the Gentiles, / to open eyes that are blind, / to free captives from prison / and to release from the dungeon those who sit in darkness."*

Isaiah 42:6-7 NIV

But when the right time came, God sent his Son, born of a woman, subject to the law. God sent him to buy freedom for us who were slaves to the law, so that he could adopt us as his very own children.

Galatians 4:4-5 NLT

See what great love the Father has lavished on us, that we should be called children of God! And that is what we are!

1 John 3:1a,b NIV

Pray

Heavenly Father, thank you for your faithful love. Thank you for sending Jesus so that I can have a relationship with you. I rejoice in your mercy and celebrate your grace. I praise you for your faithful love. Amen.

Epilogue:
A Season of Joy

Epilogue: A Season of Joy

There is no time of year like the Christmas season, when ordinary time and space are taken over by a sense of wonder and reverence and merriment. Even though Christmastime is often filled with busyness and activity and stress, at the heart of the season is joy—contagious, infectious joy. That is as it should be, for Christmas is meant to be the celebration of the one who came to give us life and set us free. Now that's a reason for joy! And no one is more joyful than God himself, because Christmas is about God getting his kids back.

In Luke 15, Jesus tells us of the Father's joy through the story of the prodigal son, a young man who is lost and found again. Bored and restless, the young man decides to leave his home and family, burning bridges as he goes. He goes off to lead the decadent life he desires; but in the end, worn out by his bad choices and failed dreams, he realizes that, in order to survive, he must go home and beg his father for forgiveness:

So he got up and went to his father.

But while he was still a long way off, his father saw him and was filled with compassion for him; he ran to his son, threw his arms around him and kissed him.

The son said to him, "Father, I have sinned against heaven and against you. I am no longer worthy to be called your son."

But the father said to his servants, "Quick! Bring the best robe and put it on him. Put a ring on his finger and sandals on his feet. Bring the fattened calf and kill it. Let's have a feast and celebrate. For this son of mine was dead and is alive again; he was lost and is found."

Luke 15: 20-24 NIV

As children of God, we have all sinned and gone our own way. Beginning in the garden, we have rejected the good things of our Father in order to pursue our own desires. Our sin separated us from God, and we couldn't make our way back to him. So God made a way for us—he sent Jesus to earth to rescue us and welcome us home as his beloved children.

On the very first Christmas Day, God was certainly joyful because he was getting his children back—his from-the-beginning rescue plan set into motion. And he couldn't contain his excitement; he had to tell someone, so he sent his angels to proclaim the good news:

There were sheepherders camping in the neighborhood. They had set night watches over their sheep. Suddenly, God's angel stood among them and God's glory blazed around them. They were terrified. The angel said, "Don't be afraid. I'm here to announce a great and joyful event that is meant for everybody, worldwide: A Savior has just been born in David's town, a Savior who is Messiah and Master. This is what you're to look for: a baby wrapped in a blanket and lying in a manger."

At once the angel was joined by a huge angelic choir singing God's praises:

Glory to God in the heavenly heights,

Peace to all men and women on earth who please him.

Luke 2:8-14 THE MESSAGE

All of heaven was rejoicing that day, for joy was birthed into the world! God, in the form of a tiny baby, was sent to rescue us all.

Through Jesus Christ, God revealed to us who he was and is. Through Jesus, we are able to joyfully receive the wonderful gift of God's love and mercy, which he is pleased to give to us.

Hallelujah! What a Savior! Because of God's great gift to us—God himself, wrapped up in Jesus—we can rejoice at Christmastime at his great love for us. We can be free to unwrap God's great gift with unabashed joy and wonder and celebration, eager to show off the wonderful gift he has given. We can run to the Father, whose arms are open wide, welcoming us home. We can heartily sing, "Joy to the world! The Lord is come!"

Reflect

Does it change your view of Christmas to think of it as God's rescue plan for getting his kids back? How can this perspective help to make your celebration even more joyful?

_____

_____

_____

_____

_____

How has "unwrapping" God in Jesus enriched your preparation for Christmas this Advent season? What can you do to share your wonder, excitement, and joy for God's wonderful gift with others?

_____

_____

_____

_____

_____

Meditate

Now the tax collectors and sinners were all gathering around to hear Jesus. But the Pharisees and the teachers of the law muttered, "This man welcomes sinners and eats with them."

Then Jesus told them this parable: "Suppose one of you has a hundred sheep and loses one of them. Doesn't he leave the ninety-nine in the open country and go after the lost sheep until he finds it? And when he finds it, he joyfully puts it on his shoulders and goes home. Then he calls his friends and neighbors together and says, 'Rejoice with me; I have found my lost sheep.' I tell you that in the same way there will be more rejoicing in heaven over one sinner who repents than over ninety-nine righteous persons who do not need to repent.

"Or suppose a woman has ten silver coins and loses one. Doesn't she light a lamp, sweep the house and search carefully until she finds it? And when she finds it, she calls her friends and neighbors together and says, 'Rejoice with me; I have found my lost coin.' In the same way, I tell you, there is rejoicing in the presence of the angels of God over one sinner who repents."

Luke 15:1-10 NIV

I delight greatly in the LORD;
*   my soul rejoices in my God.*
For he has clothed me with garments of salvation
*   and arrayed me in a robe of his righteousness,*
as a bridegroom adorns his head like a priest,
*   and as a bride adorns herself with her jewels.*

Isaiah 61:10 NIV

For the LORD your God is living among you.
  He is a mighty savior.
He will take delight in you with gladness.
  With his love, he will calm all your fears.
  He will rejoice over you with joyful songs."

Zephaniah 3:17 NLT

Pray

Loving God, thank you for loving us so much that you sent your only Son, Jesus, to rescue us. Thank you for making a way for us to come home and then welcoming us as your beloved children. Fill me with such wonder and joy and excitement about this good news that I am always eager to share it with others. May I rejoice in the precious gift of Jesus—God under wraps—not only at Christmastime but each and every day of the year. Amen.

Notes

Notes

Chapter 1: God Is Expectant

1. Robert K. Brown, Philip W. Comfort, translators, and J. D. Douglas, ed., *The New Greek-English Interlinear New Testament* (Wheaton, IL: Tyndale, 1990), 381.
2. "Paul Harvey and 'The Man and the Birds,' " Christian Heritage Fellowship, accessed February 14, 2014, http://christianheritagefellowship.com/paul-harvey-and-the-man-and-the-birds-a-christmas-story/.

Chapter 2: God Is Dangerous

1. Ehud Netzer, *The Architecture of Herod, The Great Builder* (Tubingen, Germany: Mohr Siebeck, 2006), xvii.
2. http://www.fischerarthistory.com/pietagrave.html
3. C. S. Lewis, *Mere Christianity,* (San Francisco: Harper Collins, 1980), 205.
4. Daniel Ladinsky, translator, *The Gift: Poems by Hafiz the Great Sufi Master* (New York: Penguin Compass, 1999), 187–88.
5. Eric Metaxas, *Bonhoeffer: Pastor, Martyr, Prophet, Spy* (Nashville: Thomas Nelson, 2010), 514.
6. Ibid., 139.
7. Ibid., 237.
8. Ibid., 505, 532.

Chapter 3: God Is Jealous

1. qin'ah, http://www.biblestudytools.com/lexicons/hebrew/nas
   /qinah.html

Chapter 4: God Is Faithful

1. George A. Buttrick, ed., *The Interpreter's Dictionary of the Bible*,
   "s. v. 'Jesus Christ' by F. C. Grant," (Nashville: Abingdon Press,
   1962, 1980), 869.
2.. Fyodor Dostoyevsky, *The Idiot* (1869), Part Two, chapter four.
   Public domain.

Authors

The authors of *Under Wraps* all have been part of the preaching and teaching staff of The Woodlands United Methodist Church in The Woodlands, Texas.

Jessica LaGrone served as Pastor of Creative Ministries and currently is Dean of the Chapel at Asbury Seminary. She is the author of two Bible studies, *Namesake* and *Broken and Blessed*, as well as a book based on her most recent study. She and her husband, Jim, have two young children.

Andy Nixon served as lead pastor of the contemporary worshiping community called The Loft, and currently is Development Director for Children's Safe Harbor in Montgomery County, Texas. He and his wife, Deborah, have two children.

Rob Renfroe is Pastor of Discipleship and leads the popular Quest, a men's Bible study attended by over five hundred men. He also is president of Good News, a national organization committed to the doctrinal integrity and spiritual renewal of The United Methodist Church. He and his wife, Peggy, have two adult sons.

Ed Robb is Senior Pastor. Serving the church for more than thirty years, his vision and leadership have led the church to become one of the fastest growing churches in Methodism, with over 10,000 members. He and his wife, Beverly, have three adult children.